MW01195507

REVISIONS

ERIC TRAN

SIBLING RIVALRY PRESS

LITTLE ROCK, ARKANSAS

DISTURB / ENRAPTURE

Sibling Rivalry Press, LLC
PO Box 26147
Little Rock, AR 72221

info@siblingrivalrypress.com

www.siblingrivalrypress.com

ISBN: 978-1-943977-46-8

This title is housed permanently in the Rare Books and Special Collections Vault of the Library of Congress.

First Sibling Rivalry Press Edition, February 2018

for Anna

CONTENTS

2.

REVISIONS

1

REVISIONS

Do not let him buy them, those pleated shorts, take off the cropped black wig whose strands stuck to his face, let it be unknown how many tapioca pearls he can eat in one sitting. Make us leave that grocery store, never see the salted fish or strawberry flute straws. Please, unfall the 28 days of rain. Make us skip the workout of the day, unpush, unpull. Unspeak the broken Vietnamese, silence the half conversations, dial down the laughter. I've heard yesterday is just condensation on a window, the day before an orb spider's web. The street lamp outside my apartment started to flicker but now holds strong. It can be like that. Let the tide recede, the bud unbloom. Make him step back through the doorway, make him turn the lock closed. Redact the news, those same four headlines, the bridge, the sight, the rows of flower wreaths. At least—redo the day of shopping, of him asleep on the drive home. Do not let me brake gently at any exit or stop light, let me speed and swerve. Let him startle and wake. Dear god, make him open his eyes.

BEING GONE

When I said *hospital* or *busy* I realize I was still talking and it took until this week to hear anyone else, like a friend who said this summer he got robbed in Vietnam: the thief scaled a wall and jimmied the window lock and pocketed the phone right off the bed, and he prefers to have slept, so it feels like he was *never robbed at all*, or another friend humming bluegrass in the hall, bearing coffee in the morning and whiskey in the evening, or my grandma showing me how to pray to the family's patron goddess, like how they did on the boats over to the US or when I was applying to damn med school in the first place, or Dan, the last thing he said and will ever say to me—was it *anh* for big brother or no words at all, just the signature smile and headshake—or my cousin who drives us past the airport and says my dad would take him here to watch the planes take to sky and when I start talking, always always talking, about being jealous of not seeing this side of him, only the dad with calloused hands, Johnny says, *No you were there too, you were too small to see anything, you were too young to know how to remember.*

MY MOTHER ASKS HOW I WAS GAY BEFORE SLEEPING WITH A MAN

She says I've taught you this before: press the skin
of pears to your nose to sense if they're ripe,
sound out foreign words, spring-load them on your lips

before flicking them off your tongue. Measure drinks
with your fingers, test gold with your teeth. Do you trust
the strength of ice with the weight of one toe,

the day's weather without throwing yourself into it,
the spice of a pepper by biting the tip? Son,
the world is not known by its surfaces alone.

When you cut new flowers, split their stems
like a giant vein, teach them to drink water again.
I warned you once not to touch red coils,

but you had to reach out, palm the heat,
hold the fire in your fist to learn your own fear.

ANATOMY & PHYS

Only after his suicide did we learn
Dr. Garza raped his students. I never knew
much beyond the shirtsleeves stretched

and swollen on his TAs' arms—imagine
Garza and I were similar that way.

What I learned besides my dormmate's
route to the shower, Garza's own everlasting
tan: leave the trick's address on your desk

in case you don't make it back, ride on top
if you don't trust he'll enter gently. What I didn't:

how to trace his sternal scar and say *Stop*
if he apologizes for it, how to remember
sildenafil opens vessels in the cock and slacks

muscles in the heart; where halothane strokes,
quiets a student's brainstem. And half-learned,

Garza's talk on suffocation. A body stores
acid if you don't exhale. He pulled a student
sitting in my row: *hold your breath, son.*

He did, that big chest stilled, his face rising red.
Later I'll hold lungs and marvel at their fullness

and ability to collapse. Later I'll read blood acid
levels, I'll remember I once wanted him to pick me,
and still my blood will run hot.

SOCRATIC METHOD

So student, say sinus rhythm, say sawtooth wave form—so what?
Say sine and cosine, say sweat stain, say for certain: sick or not sick
or somewhere in between. If sugars, say sliding scale, if STEMI
say statin, if stumble say CT. If desat say support, if seizure say
swordfight, if sterile, if stable, if someone else is consulting, then
sigh and breathe. If fascia say dissection, if stoma say resection.
Say stippled, say sanguine, say smell of burnt sugar. Say wheezes,
say breath sounds, say sectioned and quartered. Say shopkeep, say
sentinel node, say sorry and your patient's sobbing mother. Say
Burney's sign, say psoas, say stunted and failure to thrive. Say
sucker punch, say accident, say femur snapped right in the center.
Say sundown and Posey, say sunrise and handoff. Say suffering, say
anything, stay curious. Grab your coat, son, I'll see you tomorrow.

MY DEAREST RESIDENT BRIAN,

my assigned a med student at 6AM Brian, my Florsheims pounding the linoleum because this morning's patients are especially sick Brian, my somehow every morning this week every patient is especially sick Brian, my muttering to himself about urine outputs and losartan dosages in the hallway Brian (but lilted voice around patients, *sorry to hear you didn't sleep well Brian*), my only answers my questions if Mr. Donaldson, hemoptysis and 30-pack-year smoking habit Mr. Donaldson, has lung cancer with a grim silence, my up late writing notes Brian, my still finds time for giving advice about clinical rotations Brian, my *the only feedback so far is to lose the tie Brian*, my *I only survived med school because of my wife Brian*, my Brian with multiple pagers that you won't give to another intern because they had it last night, my still thinking about Mrs. Rodriguez's heart attack in room 33 Brian, my *I'm not scared I'll get in trouble, I'm scared she'll be hurt*, my I've never seen you take lunch so I bring you two donuts in the AM Brian, my *this day is my picture of disaster* but keeps walking towards the next room and smiles Brian, my when did your skin see sun last Brian, my does each day collapse into the next Brian, a tangle or mess of morning rounds and night calls Brian, my I hope you slept some hours last night Brian, my please hydrate Brian, my we've got news Brian, my when you finally took a break Brian, my we got the results Brian, my it's not cancer Brian, my did you hear us Brian, my wildfires can burn eucalyptus trees black and charred Brian, my but they grow back at the tree tops not at the base Brian, my did you hear us Brian, my survival is seen both in the wreckage and away from it Brian, my it's not cancer Brian, my sometimes it's not cancer, Brian, some day it's not cancer

UNTITLED (PORTRAIT OF ROSS IN LA)

Because lately all joints seem rustle and twig; rising from reclining hospital beds, from cabs and laps, some human part spills off the edges. On the worst days, the body anagrams spleen and sulcus, shine and surface. On the worst days, the body props and leans in those final selfies. Those days, the world swarms with hands—clumsy, numbed grasping for blood and breath and breast. And really no God-blessed matter can be touched and remain. No fire, no burnished doorknob. No senile woman whose head I hold still for central line placement. Not her heart's pace when we move too slow. Not her ribs snapped clean in CPR. Not your hand or mine, enclosed as the cover of a book. But if my body was dust, was subway stubs and footprints and we piled it up, would we call it healed? New, untouched? Take your palms and push—tonight, break what's left or rejoin the pieces.

DAYS AFTER ORLANDO I READ THE X-MEN

who also tried paradise once. Genosha, a mutant slave island they freed and claimed back. But even then, safety—that sugar-glass promise of dancing chainless—centered them for retribution. Issue #115, after wild sentinels with deadened eyes, after smoke and rubble, one mutant there still breathed—she turned herself hard as diamond. Giant-sized issue #1

another island: our team followed a distress call, but the mutant was the fist of earth itself. Vines and fault lines trying to crumble the buildings. Imagine—all those homes atop that grieving face. But really, any episodes they practiced wearing such dusk: #25 Iceman sculpts a doppelgänger and watches a brainwashed ally shatter that frozen dummy

formless; the friend-foe mourns so much he finally remembers his humanity. #38 Jean Grey holds her dying demon clone, who, faced with a legacy as a second-tiered loved one, kamikazes their psychic link. Last panel, she's spread supine like a bludgeoned raven. #24 Kitty Pryde phases a cosmic bullet right through Earth, but can't release the death

she's stopped. I know, metaphors, painted so thick the layers won't dry, but this all feels like web and tissue. I mean I'm still staring right into the blaring eclipse of also wanting that ungloved touch, my blue fur unmatted and combed out clean. No mutation can stop such burning. Maybe I teleport, but only via a hell dimension. Shape-shift, more wolf

and fanged than I can bear. Early on the Professor made ruby quartz glass to soothe the eyes' work—but even then the world tints redder still.

10 RESPONSES TO A CLICKBAIT HEADLINE

Australian Man Wakes From Coma Speaking Fluent Mandarin
Proving Again the Brain is a Wondrous Thing – IJReview.com

A stroke survivor makes his living touring schools with the story of his survival. He told me he could only remember nouns; for the abstract he thought in rhymes: for *this* and *there*, he pictured *kiss* and *bear*, maybe *piss* and *hair*, *mist* and *snare*.

-

In old age, the brain becomes the weakest link, the first chain to snap under duress. Insomnia, UTI, too few leafy greens can erase all the names in your family, make you think the neighbor is being kidnapped, erase the ability to know if the cats around your feet are real or imagined.

-

My friend says that when on molly, whomever you're with becomes family. *But it's all real*, she insists, *you're still close when you're sober again*. In high school, they told us MDMA burned holes in your brain, Swiss cheese in your skull. New studies show it still may cause neuro damage, but may also treat PTSD, may delete neurons but maybe the ones that hold onto violence, reflexes for balling your hands into fists.

-

I've stopped watching TV shows with violence, where characters are slammed against walls, knocked unconscious to remove them from fight scenes. I flinched each time, wondering how many concussions a person could get before they left the scene permanently.

-

Dementia patients may depend on the sun to keep them steady. In sundowning, they get confused by lengthening shadows, begin to shake and pace aimlessly, as if there wasn't enough light to remind them how to put one foot in front of the other.

-

Imagine finding your son awake from a coma, returned after months of silence. Would you cry that he talked again, or that you didn't know what he meant by *jia*, home, or *jia ting*, family?

-

Alien hand syndrome can occur after surgery to cure epilepsy. The hand can feel foreign, autonomous. It can be bratty and push away a chair you mean to pull close, or naughty and creep up your thigh while you sleep. Some patients give the hand a name and when it throws away their microwave burrito say, *Oh Henry doesn't like it when I don't eat well.*

-

A neuro professor once told me that time moves faster as you age because kids pack boxes with their toys spilling out the top and adults fold and tuck into suitcases. The brain improves with packaging, learns how to speed towards those last few days.

-

I spend a lot of time in my head thinking of synonyms, slant-definitions, things that slip around the edges. For *wondrous*, maybe miraculous like God, staggering like one drink too many. Precious like crystal glasses, sublime like looking from a mountaintop, unclear how deep the valley is below.

-

I once worked in a hospice where a husband moved in with his dying wife. He told me sometimes he stayed awake with his finger under her nose to know she was breathing. He was developing dementia himself, told me: *I just couldn't live without my wife, I mean son, no I mean my wife. My wife.*

FORENSICS LECTURE AFTER THE SHOOTING OF MICHAEL BROWN

This morning, a list of wounds to commit
to memory: contusion, abrasion, compound fracture.
There's no irony in the lecturer's voice, in her floral dress.

She says *Let's cut to the chase* and shows a wrist
flayed open to bone. She doesn't spare the shiny ligament
ribbons under the skin, the marble eyes of a lynched

woman, bed sheet noose printed with roses. No slides
about closing split scalps, for helping skin pull itself
whole. No cure for tear gas, for Tasers, for another black boy

gunned down by cops. That's her point: medicine
can't always undo the violence. The knowledge we want
is how and who. The relationship of shooter and victim's

entrance wound. At close range, you could see a face
and leave a halo of soot, of scarring and shame. At distance,
the body can be any black figure, the gun can fire a pinhole

nearly small enough to ignore. We need to examine more
because a cue stick can leave a cut on the face and blood
pooling on the brain. Reason the act to the actor,

to his synapses firing. Injury pattern, a broken
puzzle. What piece goes first? What goes last
is always a mother without her son.

Trauma is a physics equation: damage as mass pushed
by speed and momentum. It's why a sledgehammer
can splinter a shinbone, why a round of bullets

blows clean through a city. But when the who and how
are clear, the why is still a moth you want to crush in your fist.
If the narrative of a murder is mute, is molten,

you can ask an infinity of questions. Even the lecturer
evades us: picture after picture of exposed
organs, a wrench next to a canyon in a skull, no story,

no resolution. She understands the question is the answer,
the question is the weapon. It's a knife you hold
blade-first to defend yourself. Don't let it go—

if it's too late to save a life, if the question
is a blood-letting, inside bursting out, then bleed.
Let them see how red we are.

REGRETS, IN THE STYLE OF CLUE

Your ex at Home Depot with the mower
    blades and your cut off jeans, or mom
        in the dark garage, her face blossomed

plum, or teen at clinic and his chipped
pink polish, or the sober Juggalo
    at Red Cross and a matte black BB gun.

        The psychic by the door and spirits
    urging, *Trust him*. Dan on the bridge
without wallet or phone, or yourself

    on the bridge with the bag of chips.
Your coach and the veins and callous
    grip and the *No man lifts*

        because he's happy. Speech started
    and sputtered dead under the swing
of a single bulb, or the drag queen

    denude of shadow and dress with the trust
fall to bed, or from his studio the city
    behind the quilted curtains, or any black

        in your vision. Dan in the cookie aisle
    and a tin of durian straws, with the ten-speed
in the quad and floodlights, with the snap-

    back in the gyms, with a keychain,
        with the triceps, with the dumplings,
    with the train set in the snowstorm,

with the statuesque man in the city,
in the sun, in the closet, in a doorway,
in a room that smells of laundry or copper.

HOW TO PRAY

take the Eucharist / the body / the pulse / in your hand a book
/ of matches / in the other plums and potpourri / incense /
the moon / cakes your grandma sliced in eighths / a knife /
your palm / pressed to the other / draw a cross / a card / sell
your Sabbath / bargain a bull / ask for anything / but this right
now / count beads until the anger sleeps / beside you / gild
the edges / gloss and guess / gist and djinn / fast or purge /
your belongings / any tether to the sod your father laid down
/ taste the body / the crumbs and wine / what is blood but
leaves / turning season / to let the sun pass through / what is
injury but preparation / be willing / be wild / blueberries in
summer / be forgiveness / like a small dark box / be prostrate
/ be praise, an overflowing fountain / be a whistling, worried
kettle / beg *shepherd* / *savior* / *take me off the fire* / *empty me out*

UNTITLED (PORTRAIT OF ROSS IN LA)

Certain by tins

                    of keratin Calcium   strung flat

        by candy floss

                        Pulsing   homes traced

in gossamer Wrinkled

                        cellophane September

                                        frost Constant

      ledge and shimmer

                        meaning lost   soon Faith hands

familiar   to collapse

                                Trigger   and thumb

        open cotton skin

                    sighs swelled   cracked

chapped Cheap   seams Still hands

                                prints smear

      on bathroom mirrors

                    claws   through honeycomb

Take sweetness   once and more

                                With teeth

In woolen palm

                    Other hand   barring gust

from soft and beating

                    straw and kindling

2

EVERYTHING I KNOW ABOUT MY PARENTS

they never told me—My father's pocket
notebook from his youth, pages in Thai
though we are Vietnamese, cursive loops

though he can't read, bound in leather,
but he's owned none but a wallet, creased
around a single credit card. In the margins

I drafted comics when we rationed
blank paper. *Stupid*, maybe he said once,
maybe nothing at all, but I've not seen it

since. My mother worries I've known hunger,
italicized *hunger* like a foreign language,
like a thought bubble, like a socket

shorting out. Her heart missed peasant food,
I think. She never called it that, just pressed
flour into strips dropped in oil

she told me never to eat. How do I
convince you this was love? Here:
Family portrait in negative space

and grease-soaked newsprint, and me
—what have I said beyond *I'm gay*,
not *I love him*, not *I got tested*, not

another night of screaming and silence, another
emptied box of tissue, no one saying *How
will I live through this?* Portrait in humming

light bulb gone quiescent,
map of paths you cannot take.

ELOISA—

How to explain the bathhouse to you, how I buy pricey eucalyptus soap because that's what's dissolved in the steam room mist. I don't like the smell—I think it's rich fool's mint, but once a yoga instructor dotted eucalyptus oil on my temples and I was taken back to that steam room, to the shadows of bodies against mist. I thought of how to describe the appeal of anonymity of both subject and object and I stupidly thought of party mix, where no single item tastes good really, but in the context each handful feels right on your tongue. Last night, the men stood like ancient statues until one of them wandered into the corner. Without any signal other men followed one-by one, made a mass of limbs and grunts. Eloisa, I wonder if what I mean to tell you is wandering the hallways of by-the-hour rooms, waiting to catch any lingering glance, is like some sex-starved Orpheus or Theuseus chasing his bull-hung minotaur. That I found him, my lover ghost or half-beast, in the heart of the maze, sitting in the mist like a grand mountain, that he was the only man I touched that night, that he came in my mouth without warning or a move to return the gesture. Maybe what I mean to tell you is leaving the maze, minimally scathed but also prizeless, skin still hungry for warm, and stopping by the water fountain to rinse or swallow. The man walked by me, that he was still somehow a dark sylph I can't describe, that he reached out to grab my wrist and gave it a gentle squeeze goodbye.

LET ME TELL YOU ABOUT THE FIREWORKS

Since you asked what I was doing that night, or rather since you texted, *Hey let's get married,* because the Raleigh courthouse was open late to let the gays finally get hitched. Maybe I'll think *yes* but instead tell you how I just lost all three sets of tennis—the first time I've played in almost three years. I can mention the queer tennis group, but not how I'll lose half my toenails in the coming months because I'm too eager to get back in shape. But let's not get too far ahead of ourselves: second date first. We can mention how the sky is dark and pregnant with rain and storm, how I ventured onto the courts anyways and you downed pitchers of margaritas downtown, maybe I'll hobble in and out of the shower, and maybe you'll show up unexpectedly, still drunk on salt rims. Maybe I'll say *No* and maybe you'll you pin me down anyways, maybe playfully or maybe not. Maybe I'll ask you to leave and your face will be painfully, painfully quiet. But again, too far ahead. Slower. I need to tell you about those fireworks: they're like sparks flying in metal shops, only they're falling on my car idling at the stoplight. It's a shower of gold, sheets and sheets of twinkle lights and I'm tempted to lower my windows and palm a handful. Later it'll rain for real, a thunderous, flooding downpour, but I need to tell you all of us on the road are maybe so happy about tonight's victories and losses that we don't mind going slow, moving politely single file. I need to tell you everyone gets home safe.

THE FIRST X-RAY

Wilhem Roentgen aimed radiation at objects,
each holding photons like a dam holds flood.
What spilled over was cast on film, a portrait

of what was lost: a metal sheet, a set of weights,
his wife's hand—silhouette of her wedding ring.
The history of innovation cycles, a stone wheel

that hones a knife's edge. Biotech is built small
for warzones, to trace poison in water. Mustard gas
fathered chemo: autopsies of blistered victims

showed tumors lulled into slumber. Wildfires
clear stagnant fields clean—eventually you
hardly remember the earth's scarred flesh. Still,

I remember cadavers and my reluctant scalpel
baring down onto bone. I remember someone
said, *They wanted you to learn*, as if permission

could supplant the image of skin peeled out
like an onion. Roentgen saw this muddled
future; he called them X-rays, x for unknown,

but he predicted deformed fingers, twisted bowels,
and hid behind lead. Even his wife, mother
of lobar pneumonia, of excised bullets and clots,

knew her role in this play. At her naked
knuckles, she cried, *I have seen my death*,
but not once did she pull her hand away.

ALTERNATIVES TO SAYING IT

Sounds like bay door yawning open, bottle cap popped with iron rail. Sorry, sounds not like *cancer*. Nothing like *sorry*. Like hard-packed rubber, like bounce off plywood base. Knurled steel spinning—oh whistle and catch, gasp and glottal stop. Catgut kissed felted air, fat smoked across coal. River dive: crack like virgin femur, like unleavened bread. Mower blade spinning rocks, mouthful of fork and china. OK so velvet brushed napped and flat, but too no Velcro pulling free, no hooks from lines of eye. Three phone rings and answer or shrill to voicemail. Streetlight flicker: off and on, off and on, off and

TAKOTSUBO

The Japanese takotsubo (ceramic pot used to trap octopus)
has a shape that closely resembles that of the heart.
— Circulation, Volume 118, Issue 25

You thought what of these quarters

of clay and terracotta? These walls playing

indestructible, this deep, dark dwelling. Boy

you tossed this heavy hideaway overboard

and it sank like any loyal thing wants to.

Do you trust this hollowed vessel, that emptiness

which has no limits? Son, there is loss and anger

swarming and punching sure as entropy,

fight so fierce they break foundation first.

Broken open, the heart and hearth still warm

with enough fire and fuel. Place your ear

to that roar—each lick of an inside burning

itself to live. Let's see that apex, hoist that rope.

Discover what grief fills your home today.

PORTRAITS OF THE DAYS' GRIEFS

Today's grief and I grope the man I've loved while the man he's loved finds us coffee. Today's grief hurls the train not as late as forewarned, a vanishing point reversed. Some days' griefs identify in third person fem and she snaps like a neon harness, sweats like virgin leather—you can't throw these griefs in the wash. Last week's grief bleached me straw and dander then tugged patch and bald. One morning's grief bled thin down my windshield, the next day's slicked thick like jelly. I guess most grieve by grip and tread, but isn't all grief a failing brake? One day's grief gifts a red jerk-off rash, the next wants to push its dick in dry, but honey I begged spit on that kind of grief. In grief succession: seatmate quietly sings opera through turbulent sky, two apples for dinner, pocketing a pack of gum or a lady's purse or a jockstrap, I don't really care. One night's grief split my lip and sucked the wound to clot. No grief has held my body since, but still: a sting each time I kiss it goodnight.

PORTRAITS OF HANDWASHING

after Bernard Cooper

I.

Soap the backs of your hands, too. You are a pinwheel of contact points; more than your palms have touched the world today. Flood the fine creases of your wrists, bury the mountains of your knuckles. Each finger is a molting snake, each hand an unbaptized infant. Look: Your forearms end in clouds. The sink is a fresh-made bed, and your hands carry so many weary travelers.

II.

Lasse, my dorm's health educator, taught us to lather for at least two rounds of "Happy Birthday." He had a lingering Swedish accent and unironically loved the Swedish fish gummies I bought him for Christmas. *Happy birthday to you!* he sang. He sang so happily we felt like it was actually all our birthdays; his mimed lathering was our puppet show. When Lasse caressed our fevered foreheads, I imagined him later, at the sink, humming himself bright and clean again.

III.

A nurse visited our class and implored us to be vigilant: *When you enter a patient's room, when you leave.* She wanted to say, *You could save lives*, but she actually said, *You could kill people.* She waved her arms emphatically, flapped them like a bird in distress, or maybe she was just air-drying her hands. Maybe she had just washed them. Maybe her hands, which looked thick and strong even from seven rows back, had just held a pink, wailing newborn or palmed a syringe of adrenaline for another patient's stilled heart.

IV.

In New York, I know three bakers who wash their hands, their counters, their instruments before spinning together white sugar flowers. In North Carolina, my neighbor scoops lumps out of a litter box. Elsewhere, after a potter presses out a wide-mouthed bowl, a 5-year-old picks his nose. A butcher, a barehanded fisherman. Somewhere, someone on a great first date uses the bathroom and lingers in the mirror. Mouths again and again, *Oh my god. Oh my god.*

V.

Once, as a kid, I tried to make a kite out of chopsticks and printer paper, but it never caught air. When my dad got home from the mechanic shop, he sighed at my attempt. With a small grout brush, he scrubbed the oil from his hands before building me a new one. Once, he cupped a family of crickets and held them near my ear. Once, he slapped me down to kitchen tile and then iced my bruise. His kite flew above our apartment rooftop. He wanted me to hold the string, but I refused, afraid it might slip, even from a tightly clenched fist.

IF ASKED

Because stricture and scripture, because a man said ejaculating paused his prostate pain, but he was still a right Catholic otherwise. Because circumcision and circumstance, because slipping the skin can kill the right kind of hemophilic. Because death is a test result. Because we always check left vs. right before surgery. Because there are a lot of organs the size of your fist. Because an impending sense of doom follows both hemolysis and anxiety. Because my attending says he wakes to take care of the dying and by evening prays to return to his wife and kids. Because daily can mean night or day. Because the intern says *I really don't think hospitals are a place of healing.* Because ice burns, because chiaroscuro, because you knock while you open the door. Because metaphysics and metastasis, because pheo and pheno. Because a murder of crows, maybe blackbird or shadow. Because frankly hospice and hospital. Because how else do you describe your 9-year-old patient with absence seizures when every minute is the wrong one to say she's beautiful? Who do you tell about her staring spells—her eyes wide as if taking in the entire world and what she sees is why her body shakes, why still she is silent.

ANSWERS

for Kyle

You never asked, but it's overcast, it's the sky the shade of both dawn and dusk so the sun is both rising and setting, it's Schroedinger's cat on the horizon. It's burnt rice in the pot, the loose hang of a tank top's neck. It's discovering dog ear in a library book, it's knowing the most important lines of your life before you've even met them.

It's riding your bike downhill, ass out of the seat, not worried about traffic, it's the wind whistling in your ear's pinna—pure and solid. It's the sound of a pile of quarters in your pocket that your grandma gave you to get whatever you wanted at the 7-11. Hell it's any kind of money when the aunts get laid off again.

It's standing in line at the Griffith Observatory, the busiest telescope stateside, it's a handful of tourists away from seeing Jupiter, tolerating the guide who makes the same joke about each person holding the record for the most number of views at the stars, it's the little kid hogging the eyepiece because he buys into it—for every second he stretches out, he's the most special person in the world.

It's mango sliced around the pit, it's the rinds with teeth marks. It's a worn down callous, a string of green balloons. It's someone covering your eyes—*Guess who*, they say but what they're trying to ask is, *Who else could it be?*

ACKNOWLEDGMENTS

I cannot begin to name all the people who make my writing possible and sustainable. But for their hands in this project: the Travelers Club (Anna Sutton, Gabriella Tallmadge, Regina Diperna, Nathan Johnson, Whitney Ray), Zachary Doss, Ben Hoffman, Chelsea Hodson, Asher Dark, Daniel Gardner, Eloisa Amezcua, Kathy Meachem and the UNC School of Medicine Asheville Program, Ocean Vuong, and Bryan Borland and Sibling Rivalry Press.

And the editors and staff of the following journals, who published these poems, sometimes in different forms:

"Being Gone," "Eloisa—," "Let Me Tell You About the Fireworks" in *New Delta Review*, winner of 2015 *New Delta Review* Matt Clark Prose Award

"My Mother Asks Me How I Was Gay Before Sleeping with a Man" in *Voicemail Poems* and *Best of the Net 2015*

"Socratic Method" and "Takotsubo" in *Lockjaw*

"My Dearest Resident Brian," in *DIAGRAM*

"Untitled (Portrait of Ross in LA)" and "Alternatives to Saying It" in *Superstition Review*

"10 Responses to a Clickbait Headline" in *Boiler*

"Forensics Lecture After the Shooting of Michael Brown" in *The Nervous Breakdown*

"If Asked" in *Black Warrior Review*

"Answers" in *Tinderbox Poetry*

"The First X-Ray" in *Dialogist* and *Best of the Net 2015*

"Portraits of the Days' Griefs" in *The Shallow Ends*

"Portraits of Handwashing" in *The Collagist*

"Regrets in the Style of Clue" in *Figure 1*

ABOUT THE AUTHOR

Eric Tran is a medical student at the University of North Carolina and holds an MFA from UNCW. He is the author of *Affairs with Men in Suits*, and was winner of the 2015 *New Delta Review* Matt Clark Prose Award and a finalist in the 2015 *Indiana Review* 1/2K Prize and the *Tinderbox* Poetry Prize. His work appears in or is forthcoming in *Diagram, Indiana Review, Black Warrior Review, Best of the Net*, and elsewhere.

ABOUT THE PRESS

Sibling Rivalry Press is an independent press based in Little Rock, Arkansas. It is a sponsored project of Fractured Atlas, a nonprofit arts service organization. Contributions to support the operations of Sibling Rivalry Press are tax-deductible to the extent permitted by law, and your donations will directly assist in the publication of work that disturbs and enraptures. To contribute to the publication of more books like this one, please visit our website and click *donate*.

Sibling Rivalry Press gratefully acknowledges the following donors, without whom this book would not be possible:

Liz Ahl

Stephanie Anderson

Priscilla Atkins

John Bateman

Sally Bellerose & Cynthia Suopis

Jen Benka

Dustin Brookshire

Sarah Browning

Russell Bunge

Michelle Castleberry

Don Cellini

Philip F. Clark

Risa Denenberg

Alex Gildzen

J. Andrew Goodman

Sara Gregory

Karen Hayes

Wayne B. Johnson & Marcos L. Martínez

Jessica Manack

Alicia Mountain

Rob Jacques

Nahal Suzanne Jamir

Bill La Civita

Mollie Lacy

Anthony Lioi

Catherine Lundoff

Adrian M.

Ed Madden

Open Mouth Reading Series

Red Hen Press

Steven Reigns

Paul Romero

Erik Schuckers

Alana Smoot

Stillhouse Press

KMA Sullivan

Billie Swift

Tony Taylor

Hugh Tipping

Eric Tran

Ursus Americanus Press

Julie Marie Wade

Ray Warman & Dan Kiser

Anonymous (14)

.

9 781943 977468